Annus Poeticus

Michelle Farran

Annus Poeticus

a year in verse

Annus Poeticus: a year in verse
ISBN 978 1 76041 699 7
Copyright © Michelle Farran 2019

First published 2019 by
Ginninderra Press
PO Box 3461 Port Adelaide 5015 Australia
www.ginninderrapress.com.au

Contents

Introduction	11
8: An Italian Affair	13
9: Midsummer Days	14
16: Eddie's Shed	15
17: Looking into the Land	16
22: Cows	18
23: Awaiting the Storm	19
27: Wine and Good Company	20
28: Rushing	21
29: Student-free Day	22
30: The General Store	23
31: Long and Winding Road	24
32: Homecoming	25
33: Small Country Schools	26
35: Feeding Children	27
39: Three Ravens	28
40: Burbia	29
41: Driving Country Roads	30
42: ASD and Feeling	31
44: The Pull	32
46: The Birthday Party	33
47: Zen and the Tractor	34
51: This Sacred Vessel	35
52: Revisiting Memories	36
55: Pedagogy – The Pleasure of Inspiring Learning	37
56: Missing Someone	38
57: Swimming Lessons	39
58: The Country Talent Quest	40
59: Candle	41
61: The RSL Club	42

62: The Child Cave	43
63: Time to Think	44
65: Wind on the Monaro	45
67: Small Town Show	46
70: Too Tired to Dance	48
84: How Hard It Is	49
85: The Damaged Kids	50
86: An Island of Time	51
87: Cider Clock	52
88: Entitlement	53
90: Easter	54
98: Book	55
99: The Visitor	56
103: Small Blessings	57
106: Damaged	58
109: The Small Gestures	59
110: The Wedding Dress on the Door	60
111: Faux pas	61
112: Being Friends with an Aspie	62
113: ANZAC	63
114: Invigoration	64
115: Still Grey	65
116: Newton's Third and Aspergers	66
117: Small Hauntings	67
119: The Stick	68
120: Abuse	69
123: Navigating	70
128: Shearers Have No Bums	71
129: Flossie	72
131: Gradually the Evening Gathers In	73
132: The 'Arse-end' of Driving	74
137: Blanche and Maude	75

139: Cold	76
142: Meltdown	77
143: Warm Water	78
144: Ants In Their Pants	79
149: Sleeping On a Mountain Top	80
153: Opportunist	81
161: My Bath – My Office	82
162: The Clearing Sale	83
164: Time to Think	84
171: The Salve	85
172: Machismo	86
174: Human Frailty	87
177: Aspie Life in a Medication Age	88
182: Asperger's	90
184: Simone de Beauvoir	91
186: Sewing Lesson	92
189: Morris on Gay Marriage	93
190: Catharsis of Truth	94
196: The Call of Wild Things	95
197: The Flip Side of Adrenalin	96
203: Damaged Goods	97
205: Joy	98
207: Beards	99
211: Partnership	100
212: Disneyfied	101
213: The Solemnity and Reverence of Falling Snow	102
214: The Off Switch	103
216: Delayed Gratification	104
219: Strained Relations	105
221: Made by Hand	106
225: Sanctuary	107
228: Resolution	108

232: Blue versus Grey	109
233: Sometimes You Just Stop	110
235: The Wombat	112
239: The Gang	113
240: Third	114
242: Optimism of a Sunny Day	115
244: Of This Town	116
247: Ski Resorts	117
248: The Hottie	118
249: Changing Tack	119
251: Chris the Sheep	120
254: Homes for under 100k	121
259: The Fragility of the Human Ego	122
260: Some Compartments of my Life	123
261: The Aftermath	124
262: The Grazier's House	125
263: The Benefits of Solitude	126
269: Billie-Grace Car Washing Service	127
272: The Tough Nut	128
275: The Buzz	129
276: Nature Girl	130
279: The Songwriter	131
280: Pissing in his Pocket	132
282: He's Crying	133
285: The Scouts and the Witches	135
286: The Wave	136
287: Don't Settle for Less	137
290: I Should be Sleeping	138
292: In Bed in the Afternoon	139
294: My Tribe	140
295: The Reassurance of Hills	141
296: Time to Fish	142

297: Leave the Water on – An Ode to the Bathtub	143
299: To My Aspie Wife	144
300: Beltane Lost	146
301: Fledglings	147
306: The Date	148
308: Shades of Love	149
309: I Know I Love You Because I Miss You	150
311: Being Moved	151
315: On Dogs and Some Men	152
319: The Daisies	154
320: The Subtleties of Misogyny	155
321: Intimacy	156
323: Shut Down	157
324: And They Walked	158
325: Broken	159
326: She Just Didn't Love Him	160
330: Holding On	161
331: The Casual Affair	162
335: The Swag	163
338: Humanity on Parade	164
347: My Fergie	165
349: Christmas Beetles	166
351: Procrastination or Disorganisation?	168
353: Packing	169
356: Heat	170
357: The Art of Delayed Gratification	171
358: My Cup Runneth Over	173
363: Something Missing	174

Introduction

On our hobby farm on the edge of the Monaro, my husband Matthew and I raise children (I have eight, though only five remain at home), sheep, goats, chooks, pigs, a milking cow, fruit and vegies. To support this enterprise I am a teacher at the remotest school in Victoria (if anywhere in Victoria is truly remote).

In 2015, I set myself the challenge of composing a poem each day for the calendar year, so I wrote 365 poems in 365 days.

Now three years on, what to do with this collection which at that time was such an important way of chronicling my life?

My husband suggested that I do a cull and make a collection of the better poems. He went through and graded them (because he is also a teacher), giving an arbitrary score from A to C. These are the As.

8: An Italian Affair

It's the zing on the tongue,
And tang of aged cheese.
Indescribable,
That lingering sensation
That is garlic.
Nutty masculine essence of a European forest.
Fresh and moist.
It's the sweet, sharp aroma that sends my mind,
Wine dampened,
To sun-drenched Mediterranean hills.
Subtly citric,
Extra virgin.
Grind, grind, grind…
Inhale…
Mmmmmm
The creation of fresh basil pesto.

9: Midsummer Days

Too, too hot,
On these midsummer days.
My children are inside retreating from the scorch.
For a while they read in various contortions of repose.
Then precariously they play a card game.
Until inevitably competition causes tears and fists of retribution.

Then outer clothing is replaced by splendid embellishments.
Expressive dancers slink to the beat of an 80s crooner.
Two fairies and a ninja live in an elaborate, fantastical world
Of their own creation.

On goes the pump to water the garden.
In knickers, jocks and singlets,
Ear piercing squeals join the chorus of the petrol motor.
The shock of cold water on warm skin is too much.

16: Eddie's Shed

Like a well-worn pair of hand-knitted socks, with the heels darned,
The woolshed has the homespun beauty of simple objects.
Like the board and wool room floor,
The rickety home-made wool table is tarnished
With the grime of lanolin.
It has a soft surface that creates a subtle resistance
To palm or footfall.
Table legs are squared,
One with a brick.
Another with broken palings.
Uneven floor sunken,
And in parts missing.
This makes sweeping the locks a challenge.
In pertinent places ancient nails,
Driven into beams,
Hold packs for stain and skin pieces.
Looking like sagging matrons in middle age,
The wool bins for AAAM, Tender and Coloured fleece,
Are almost dowdy with their lack of symmetry,
Bulging in places – generally misshapen.
The odours of sheep and their excrement are not overpowering;
They mingle, complimenting the eau de cologne
Of men's sweat, stale cigarettes and kelpie.
The next run begins,
As does the music,
Loud!
And Slim Dusty has joined us,
As the Ringer from the Top End.

17: Looking into the Land

I write this poem and I know I look toward a view,
Which a Kurnai family looked out upon
Not so long ago,
Although theirs more obscured by trees.

I know this from the tools they left behind.
I find them when I dig out potatoes,
Or make a new hole for a fence post.
Stones fashioned with sharp edges.
Worn river stones with ground indentations.
Also small lumps of red clay-stone.
Completely misplaced in their habitat of quartz and granitic sand.

Sometimes I feel pleasantly haunted.
I imagine people's song,
In the swirling, rustling of forest leaves.
I think about them as I walk,
Mindfully.
I can imagine them singing their country,
Their footfalls in unison with their beating hearts,
Like my own.

It is said,
This valley means possum.
In my mind I see,
Mothers in possum-skin cloaks,
Their babies bundled snugly on their backs.
The Kurnai are coastal people,
But our valley stands on a 'way'.
A well walked route to the higher Monaro plains.

I like to dream and draw,
The ancient earth creatures
Said to inhabit this land;
Dimbulan, Dulagar, Nyol, Bagini.
They enliven my imagination.

I feel enriched by this place,
And all I survey.

22: Cows

Don't you just love cows?
Their large heads.
Dark docile eyes,
With curling eyelashes.
Their interest in your activities.
They casually saunter over to check you out.
Bulk moving on dainty toes,
Large painted nails.
The warm belly against your cheek as you milk.
Swish, swish into the bucket.
Their gangly calves with sandpaper tongues.
And swirls in their soft coats.
Tottering warily about you.
One eye on escape.

23: Awaiting the Storm

Oppressive.
Humidity and heat.
Brain-crushing air pressure.
Invisible forces aiding gravity to drag…
Drag you down.
With all the plans you had for the day.
You watch them go down the drain,
Along with your desires, good intentions, optimism and energy.
The afternoon crawls at the same pace as you complete your chores.
The pressure in your head reaches a climax.
And just when you feel you can endure it no longer,
Something breaks.
It arrives with gentle rumblings,
Darkening skies and welcome, restorative breeze.
Two black cockatoos pass overhead,
Harbingers,
Squaaaawking at intervals.
Now is the time to sit on the veranda and await the majesty
Of the storm.

27: Wine and Good Company

The warm aromas greet you at the door.
Caramelising flesh, sweetness of fresh greens.
Drop your bags and take a seat ringside.
Effervescent sparkles hit your glass.
Introductory and catch up conversation:
Smiles and questions,
Gossip,
Platter brimming,
Anticipation building,
Each portion served,
Toasts made.
Then we dine,
Conversation flows smoothly as wine.

28: Rushing

I
Rush, rush, rush!
Tightly coiled spring
Potential energy about to break out
Without purpose
Adrenalin pumped
High focus
Poor judgement
Energy quickly spent
Like a blown-out candle.

29: Student-free Day

Today was a student-free day.
Student free, but not of course teacher free.
Conversation less restrained.
No packed lunch.
Holiday stories exchanged.
Timetables adjusted, and curriculum planned.
Enrolments speculated.
Managing recalcitrant and demanding parents?
Strategies discussed.
Lessons and excursions organised.
Resources located.
Post opened.
Classrooms readied
And in your mind's eye,
As you are driving home,
You see them before you,
With eager faces and new uniforms,
Your students.

30: The General Store

It's the beating heart.
Not racing so much these days.
Ever evolving.
Has become the butcher, newsagency, fruit barn, bank,
and recently post office.
It stands almost alone.
The blank faces of the closed businesses look on,
Display windows of dust and dead blowies.
The bustling activity inside is a welcome sign of life.
Shoppers and staff welcome each other
With genuine interest and affection
Service is paramount.
The stock on the shelves reflects individuals' tastes:
Colgate, Heinz, Chum and Peck's Anchovette,
And decreases at the same rate as the population.
To shop here is to embrace your community.
Yet there are those,
Feigning poverty,
Who empty their petrol tanks to get to Aldi.

31: Long and Winding Road

Car travel,
Long repeated journeys,
Over remembered corrugations.
Potholes and blind corners,
Wildlife hot spots.

The car filled with detritus of unemployed children:
Wrappers, hair ties, odd socks, empty water bottles
And discarded toys.
Chorus from the backseat:
'What town is this?
Are we stopping here?'

Your mind wanders,
As do your eyes into a stranger's life.
Till a close call with oncoming traffic,
Draws your attention abruptly back.

You think through the day,
Your week, your life.
Rerun or plan discussions in your head.
You try to keep your eyes focused,
Ignore their drooping fatigue.

Prolonged travelling,
This is the tiring reality
Of those who choose to live in the bush.

32: Homecoming

Filled to the brim with social engagement,
Bad food, and the stimulation of new places.
My children regroup in the three-hour car journey.
A few grizzles on route.
The odd altercation.
Generally quiet resting prevails.
Then arrival,
Slowly pile out dishevelled,
From a car of disorganised detritus.
Then the loathsome job of unpacking when you are tired.
But the kids;
Well, like I said,
'Regrouped!'
Ready to start the party.

33: Small Country Schools

We are more like big families.
With our solidarity and our feuds.
We have our cliques, big fish in small ponds,
Sibling rivalry, jealousy, pettiness,
And the school-gate mafia.
And sometimes everyone is just…
Too close.
The teachers know just…
Too much.
Unpaid social workers.
More time counselling than teaching.
Yet in a small school,
They can cut through the process time.
And each child is taught as an individual.
Teachers know them almost as their own children.
In these small towns,
Country schools are the establishment, the authority.
We are the community.
Kill us off or let us die,
And there goes the community.

35: Feeding Children

Provide farm fresh:
Milk straight from the cow,
Chops and sausages from our sheep and pigs.
Clean clear water straight from heaven.
But
Garden-fresh vegetables,
Zucchini,
Broccoli,
Tomatoes,
Beans,
And all you hear is,
'Yucky!'
'Do I have to eat it to get dessert?'
'Disgusting – you know we hate…'
…Just about anything green, remotely spicy
Or with any flavour at all.

The disappointment of feeding children.

39: Three Ravens

Three Australian ravens,
One on each post.
Looking across
A Monaro pastoral idyll.
In the late afternoon,
They sit still as sentinels.
What care they for the hubbub of the 21st century?
The day is mild and the food plentiful.
They have no better occupation.
I ask you,
What is contentment?

40: Burbia

I've been in Burbia,
Seas of rooftops.
A constant buzz buzz of human activity.
Cars, kids, mowers, music and TV sets up loud.
Chubby people – baggy shorts, tight tees and trackies –
wander oblivious,
Their attention on their mobile devices.
Cars drive fast.
No courtesy, no acknowledgement.
Beep, beep, beep,
And the one-finger salute.
Feeding time:
They gorge at McDonalds.
Ignoring toddlers in the undercover playground.
Chubby children entertained by iPads.
Mum and Dad chat on Facebook,
Hundreds of friends.
Everyone seems to be ignoring each other.
Except…
When they have a 'funny kitten' video they can share.

41: Driving Country Roads

Country roads are measured in hours.
Monotony broken by the quick wave.
A simple, polite finger lift from the steering wheel.
And the sometimes unknown but usually known driver
Passes by.
A sign of solidarity.
Acknowledgement that the journey is inevitably long,
And perilous.
Dirt roads furrowed and corrugated.
Pot holes and fallen trees.
Dusk bringing kangaroos and wallabies.
Darkness – wombats stunned by the headlights.
But in that one simple human act,
We know that we are in this together.

42: ASD* and Feeling

How do you explain that you
Feel too much.

All your waking day,
You put up walls to help insulate you.
So you can function,
As you are 'typically' supposed to.
But behind that wall,
The turbulent miasma
Of emotional experience builds.
If there is not a slow release of pressure,
When you can,
Under control,
In solitude,
Slowly let those overwhelming waves come in,
And gently wash over you,

You drown.
In the rushing waterfall,
Screaming and yelling and fighting till the end.

Or in self-imposed silence.

---

* ASD: autism spectrum disorder, a developmental disorder that affects communication and behaviour.

44: The Pull

When you are up early,
Feeding-out and fencing.
The weather mild,
And everything a picture
Of rural idyll.
That is when the feelings of being torn begin.
Between your 'away from farm' work life.
That pays for life's necessities,
And this simpler existence.
Grounded, practical and life-affirming.
How it should be.

46: The Birthday Party

She strove for excellence
As close to perfection as she could get with one week
Of preparation to execute.
Identifying appropriate recipes.
Acknowledgement that a sit-down meal would not work
With the number of guests.
Finger-food.
That would work as long as it was real food.
Beautiful, tasty, unique and easily carried and held in the hands.
Exotic, but not too spicy.
Or challenging to an unused palate.
Vegetables, aquatic and terrestrial meats.
Pre-prepared and warmed in the oven or quickly roasted
On the barbecue.
Then dessert.
Not too heavy with a rich chocolate birthday cake to follow.
Fresh fruit.
Berries in season.
Drinks?
People are welcome to bring their own.
An assortment of exotic fresh fruit punches.
Alcohol of various intensities.

This was what greeted us at the most thoughtfully prepared party
I ever attended.
It was sublime food as mindful as analytic meditation.
And true art.

47: Zen and the Tractor

It is not that you drive the tractor.
It is that you fully experience each moment of driving the tractor.
The tension in your thigh as you push down and double clutch.
The force of the key against your fingers held before ignition,
Mentally count to twenty to warm the glow plug.
A cough and you release your hand,
Ignition realised.
The unity of acceleration and release.
The posture that allows you to sit fully in the seat and
   maintain concentration.
Listen to the engines song as it labours up each hill.
Enter the exact moment when you decelerate
And gently apply the brakes.
Notice the lie of the land.
Look for every obstacle, hole, tree stump.
And memorise the exact point where that baby hare
Scrabbled slowly away through the grass.
Drink when you are thirsty.
Gauge when you think that more fuel might be needed.
Navigate the land so that needless traversing is minimised.
Feel the wind in your hair and the warmth of the sun.
Smell the fresh cut grass,
And peppermint eucalyptus as you slash a misplaced shrub.
Realise that there is nowhere else in this moment you should be,
But on this little red Fergie tractor, slashing.

51: This Sacred Vessel

Notice.

In each moment,
All that it is.

The great,
Elderflower champagne.

The modest,
A hardboiled egg.

The intrinsic beauty of everyday objects,
My red Fergie tractor.

The joy in the simplicity of activities labelled mundane,
Warm dishwater.

Let all of your senses be attuned,
Eau de cologne of wet dog.

Be truly present.

Then you will appreciate this precious life –
And the sacred vessel in which you travel.

52: Revisiting Memories

It was just an underpass,
Rusted,
From a long-defunct railway line,
On an obscure dirt track,
Which had at one time,
Been the main road,
To Nimmitabel.
But many winters ago,
Almost fifteen,
This was where we had held each other,
For the first time,
After a long time parted,
At a particularly crucial stage in our,
Relatively young relationship.

Here under this bridge,
On that cold, dark, drizzly night,
When I was shivering
With stress and trepidation
At the consequences
I knew would inevitably follow,
You held onto me.

Just as you did today.

55: Pedagogy – The Pleasure of Inspiring Learning

It is not teaching that I do,
Rather
Facilitate learning.
Encourage an emotional attachment in my diminutive scholars.
If not in what they discover,
But in my own excitement for each subject.
For example;
In expressing the unfathomable patterns of written English.
I want them to feel sympathy for all the letters that
Make up their words.
To understand how letters react as they come together.
'E' is so bossy making those vowels say their name.
And 'h' has such a calming influence on 's', 't' and 'p'.
And how numerals combine magically in tens,
Just like our fingers and toes.
The wonderful patterns when multiplying 9, and 11,
And the mystery of pi.
I don't impart knowledge and facts,
Like horrible medicine that can only be regurgitated,
With little understanding or application.
No, I embrace the role of pedagogue
And feel that it is the practice of my art
To inspire wonder.

56: Missing Someone

Not such a heavy weight,
More a soft tugging
Within the cavity of your chest.
A feeling of concern,
And hope too,
That things are going well.
When your mind drifts to their image.
And you can sense them.
But you cannot see them face to face,
To be reassured.
It is whispered,
Not all encompassing.
Life's responsibilities drown it out.
But it still comes,
In the quiet moments,
The anxiety,
For those you care for,
Who are absent.

57: Swimming Lessons

The water in the wood heated pool may have been
Twenty-seven degrees Celsius,
The outside air temperature definitely was not.
Overcast with a moderate breeze,
The bathers all dangly legs and arms braved the conditions,
Enjoying the comparative warmth the water afforded.
They frolicked and porpoised,
Backstroked haphazardly in undefined directions,
Splashed, spluttered and gingerly put screwed-up faces in…
Momentarily.
Squeals of delight and the odd whinge;
'He hurt me.'
'Yes, but he hit me with the kick board.'
And then the lower lips start convulsing and turning blue.
Tremors rack the little bodies,
With little stores of body fat for insulation.
It is time to reboot in the warm showers.
The motley crew trundles off with oversize towels
And uniforms dragging.
More squeals as cool flesh greets warm water.
Chattering as damp bodies are thrust into reluctant clothes.
Then follows the intermittent parade out of change rooms,
Only to have final inspection on the concourse.
Bedraggled, with lolly bags clasped more tightly than their clothes,
They slowly amble out in friendly gaggles onto the waiting bus.

58: The Country Talent Quest

It's that time of year again
Yeah haw!
The annual Country Music Talent Quest time.
So it's out with the sheet music,
Google chords and lyrics,
And check out all the versions,
Of the best country has to offer on You Tube.
Finding the right key for junior cowgirls and boys.
Practising and getting decked in just the right kit.
Then there's the dry run on club night.
Haggling over what sections to enter.
Sleepovers for other young hopefuls,
Who tag along with your family singers.
The comedy skits and the last-minute dummy spits.
These culminate in a long long day at the local RSL.
Bring along a blanket, some books and colouring in,
To keep all ages occupied.
The smell of the make-up and hairspray.
The frocks, boots and bulging love handles.
The singers and the ear splitters.
The blood and the tears.
Wholesome entertainment for the whole family.

59: Candle

A candle lit at both ends,
Despite its beauty,
Ability to lighten a darkened space,
And provide solace when the lights have gone out.
Is likely –

Even if the utmost care and precision is taken in its lighting,
Minimising all assessed hazards
And making your best possible effort

– To burn your backside.

Yet we persist.

61: The RSL Club

Social mainstay of this country town.
Bistro meals, raffles and the odd band.
Wednesday-night schnitzels.
Upstairs is the boardroom.
Amongst the orange vinyl spinning chairs are the relics,
The glass cases of old uniforms and military paraphernalia.
The walls are inhabited by past presidents in the photographic,
And clothing styles of their respective reigns;
Black and whites with suits and brill cream,
Gaudy colour with wide ties and flares.
In the little auditorium the annual events are hosted.
High school formals, dance concerts, Melbourne Cup luncheons,
And of course Anzac and Remembrance Day commemorations.
It is friendly and familiar,
And available.
Membership is reasonably priced,
And it makes you feel a part of something bigger than yourself.

But I still hate the pokies.

62: The Child Cave

They screech and chatter like monkeys.
Whoops and calls of unbridled infant revelry.
We have paused at a town playground.
Modern play equipment in bold primary colours is ignored.
Rather, the children have discovered the steam-powered
Grader and stationary engine,
Over which they clamber unperturbed by the lack of soft fall.
Excited primates in darkened hedge habitat.
They clamber over low branches and find their secret nesting spots.
Hide and wait in excited apprehension of discovery.
When found, their silence is broken by peels of screeching joy,
No longer contained.

63: Time to Think

It seems that thinking is a dying pursuit.
Pondering, daydreaming or inviting free-flowing flights of fancy.
Lives are filled with activity.
Some purposeful, some mere distraction.
Time without activity is characterised as boring.
Now our children are spending every waking moment
Entertained or stimulated.
Their time organised into activities.
Interspersed with babysitting by screens.
All but gone is the wandering about outside,
Letting the curiosities of life bump into you.
Pleasantly poking, prodding and pondering.
We adults are no better incessantly rushing,
Or playing on our electronic devices.

Grant me time to think.

65: Wind on the Monaro

The tussocks roll,
Like an invisible hand stroking the soft fur of a puppy,
Or choppy waves on a bay.
It is soothing to watch.
It caresses my eyes.
I can observe, insulated in the sanctuary of my warm vehicle.
The stands of trees I pass are another matter,
Ferocious in their calisthenics.
They bend, whip and quake alarmingly.
I prefer to watch the grass.
Then I come upon a gang of white-winged choughs.
They are on the road, sheltering in a cutting.
As I approach they simultaneously rise in the air.
The blast they meet, causes them to rise slowly,
And make a gentle backwards arc.
Flashes of white break up the black.
They arch their backs unnaturally,
Back-paddling into the sky.

67: Small Town Show

You HAVE to go to the show…
No arguments!
To justify the gargantuan effort,
Perpetually put in,
By always the same volunteers.
See the artistic projects,
Collected over the whole year,
By class teachers at the local school.
The produce, cooking, wool, photography and artistic items.
Enjoy traditional lunch prepared by the Hospital Auxiliary.
Small daughters on small ponies,
To be led around the show ring,
Marvel at the Great Zamboni,
Comedy magician.
Visit stands representing all the emergency agencies.
The jumping castles, lolly and weaponry-filled show bags.
Packs of lolly-hyped small boys,
With plastic sub-machine guns,
Terrorising their sisters.
Over-coiffed and make-upped tweens,
Vying for Miss Showgirl.
(Who don't risk entering, for fear of losing face.)
Smart dressed farmers in moleskins, plaid shirts and hats,
Check out the various species of stock,
And the sheep dog trials.

And after a long and fatiguing day,
You pack up your tired, ratty kids,
Who clasp their ribbons, sashes, rosettes and sub-machine gun.
Then drive your familial circus,
Car with horse float,
Home.
You can let the feeling of relief wash gently over you,
Because it is over for another year.

70: Too Tired to Dance

Miss Five in her oversized school uniform,
Bag almost as big as herself,
Trundles out the school gate.
I hold her hand,
Which emerges from a rolled jumper sleeve,
Also too big.
Happily she climbs into the car,
Chatting continuously of her day,
She attempts to remove her shoe.
She should be concentrating on the seat belt.
I hurry her because we do not have time to spare.
The banter continues.
We are all buckled in and ready to go to dance lessons.
Miss Six, the bigger sister and veteran of year one,
Shares her day's happenings.
I hear no other sound from Miss Five,
Bar the heavy breathing of slumber.
The day has been too big,
Life too full and interesting,
And we are too tired to dance.

84: How Hard It Is

I feel them welling up,
Stinging my eyes.
The tears that will have to come.
Not now,
Not in this public place,
Nor in the car in front of the kids,
But in that private place
That sanctuary.

The cause?
Embarrassment and awkwardness,
Social blunder,
In front of colleagues who have no clue,
How hard it is,
And how hard I try,
To behave as they do.
I look like them,
But don't think like them.
ASD.

85: The Damaged Kids

The damaged kids cry and cry and cry.
You ask them to do some writing.
They cry and cry and cry.
The damaged kids cling.
They want to sit all over you.
Get jealous if you don't choose them
For the first go.
The damaged kids are defiant.
Push the envelope,
And cross the lines in the sand.
The damaged kids lie.
They live in a fantasy of deceit,
Better than their real world.
The damaged kids are taut
Like springs,
They snap.
But as their teacher I remind myself,
The damaged kids are still kids,
Just damaged.

86: An Island of Time

In the maddening rush of life,
Busy with matters of consequence,
And inconsequence,
We do not make an island of time to:
Stop!
Think for pure enjoyment.
Meditate.
Love each other,
And ourselves.
Switch off and tune out.
Do absolutely nothing.
Be grateful.
Pray.
Dream.
Feast all of our senses.
Be present with our family,
And friends.
Or just rest.
May every person take one day each week and find
Their island of time.

87: Cider Clock

Blop, blop, blop!
Time is measured in my kitchen,
By the
Blop, blop, blop!
Cider slowly fermenting.
Gases gradually expanding out the air-lock.
I know that eventually it will slow,
And when I come to bottling.
There shall only be the
Tock, tock!
Of the kitchen clock,
To remind me of mortality.

88: Entitlement

I have discovered a trait of the moderately wealthy,
Those who mainly,
And I mean mainly,
Derive their wealth by their own endeavours.
They justify frivolous expense on a certain,
Sense of entitlement.

Those who have not managed to climb as they have,
Are scorned as worthless, lazy,
Parasitic even.
The moderately wealthy thinking:
'Why should our hard-earned taxes be spent on this human detritus
When these people waste their unearned money
On pokies, cigarettes and alcohol?
Their kids run wild and vandalise public property.
They have no respect or common decency.
They are ungrateful,
The unentitled.'

Yet those self-congratulatory fortunate,
Whom wealth has chosen to smile upon,
Perhaps should reflect on this trait,
And recollect that they were most likely blessed,
To be born with the opportunities,
Of privilege, education and functioning families.
And that by the grace of whichever god they recognise,
Go they.

90: Easter

It is Easter in the Southern Hemisphere.
Children go to school in their
Chick and bunny Easter bonnets.
They colour in,
And search for chocolate eggs.
The weather is cooling.
Daylight saving, in its death throws seems ridiculous.
We antipodeans celebrate the coming of spring.
Yet my chickens have almost ceased laying.
I am gathering firewood for winter.
The last of the harvest,
The quinces, are being processed.
It is as bizarre as snow-covered Christmas cards.

98: Book

I take in long drafts of the familiar smell,
Paper and fresh print.
Hear the crack of the paperback's spine.
Feel the texture,
Of not quite smooth paper,
Beneath my resting hand.
The grease of my fingers,
Provide just enough friction to turn a page.
Everything is crisp and new.
Unspoiled, untainted.
I love the entirety of this sensual, tactile experience.
The opening of a new book.

99: The Visitor

We have a visitor today.
My children's madness begins subtly.
They actually help to tidy their rooms
In anticipation.
Once everything is prepared they became fractious.
When is he coming?
Distraction comes in baking sugary offerings,
Drawing and colouring,
Or finding a quiet corner to continue reading.
Then at last ten minutes before expected,
The car comes up the drive.
Kisses and embraces and presents distributed.
The volume gets louder.
After a cup of tea and chattering conversations,
The visitor and mass of children retire to the lounge room.
Then the wild rumpus really begins.
The climbing, the dressing up, the dancing about to loud music.
Voices becoming more shrill as the excitement builds.
Then there are the minor squabbles, tears and retribution.
One returns to a quiet corner to continue reading.

We have a visitor and my children go crazy.

103: Small Blessings

I recline in my sickbed and
Tap, tap these keys.
This poem writes itself on my laptop screen.
In the kitchen, my husband
Is scrubbing a pot.
I hear the sound of scourer on metal.
He has already fed us,
Organised the children and retired them to their beds.
The fire has been lit,
By him.
The house, like my heart is warming.
This rest is easy,
I don't feel his efforts
As any weight of obligation.
He takes such care of me.
These are the small blessings
Enjoyed by someone who is loved.

106: Damaged

It is not their fault,
Or anyone's,
It runs through the generations,
Passed on from parent to child,
Hurt and ignorance,
Lack of modelling,
Low expectations,
Poor self-image,
Unhelpful strategies
For coping with all that life throws,
And then passed down,
Like a terrible legacy.

109: The Small Gestures

It is in the small gestures,
The daily acts of kindness,
The patience,
And selflessness,
The notice of the needs of another,
That we should be measured.

It is in true empathy
That accepts
That we are all flawed,
And do not mean,
Out of spite,
To pass on our suffering.

These are the acts
Which define our humanity.

110: The Wedding Dress on the Door

Silk, linen, taffeta and brocade,
Beaded and bejewelled,
Of every shape, size and vintage,
On each of a hundred front doors,
Hangs a wedding gown.
A simple sign of compassion and solidarity,
A poignant gesture
For the girl who tragically
Will never become a bride.

111: Faux pas

Despite all my best efforts,
The faux pas, it seems,
Cannot be avoided.
Born of nervousness,
It blossoms out of awkwardness,
Fertilised by context blindness,
And is watered
By the accumulating, blundering, attempts to make amends.
It is inevitable,
When you have ASD.

112: Being Friends with an Aspie*

We can look a real friend in the eye.
They know that we are in earnest when we speak,
And accept our quirks,
Even if they do not always like or understand them.
They will try hard not to manipulate us
And will stand by us when we are scorned by others.
They understand that
Our motivations may be self-absorbed
But we are not malicious.
Real friends are gentle
When we are fragile.
They speak clearly and concisely,
And try not to use confusing body language.
When we waffle on,
They remind us respectfully.
They don't roll their eyes and feign interest.
They try never to leave us confused.
Aspies are loyal and true,
But we take a huge gamble
When investing in a friend.

---

* An aspie is one who has Asperger's Syndrome, which is believed to be part of the autism spectrum.

113: ANZAC

I listened, and my eyes could not resist
The squeezing pressure of unbeckoned tears;
My chest, the choking breathlessness
That another's distress invokes involuntarily.
The constable in impeccable blue chokes on the words,
Pauses to regain composure and reads
A diary entry from an ANZAC,
His Great Grandfather Dudley,
Who just over one hundred years ago tramped the same street
On which I now stood listening.
Dudley was there at the first,
0430: 25 April 1915: ANZAC Cove.
He writes of the solemn trepidation as they prepare to disembark.
The quiet.
They fix bayonets.
Then as the operation commences the ear-splitting racket
Of shelling and Lizzie's guns
He is in the boat and sees ahead the cliffs in the dawn light.
He feels the fear and excitement.
They will be the first Australians to land and fight on foreign soil.

Already they are dying around him.
Seven men hit in his boat,
The neighbouring sunk and men in the brine.
His boat hits the rocky shore.
They disembark and he is up to his neck.
Somehow he clambers ashore.
His first sight the ragged piles of dead comrades
Still warm and without the opportunity,
After all the months of training,
To fire a single shot at the enemy.

114: Invigoration

What is it about the combination of wind, rain and outdoor activity
That causes such invigoration of the soul?
I was very tired,
Up far too late last night.
Yet,
Being out in the paddock,
Moving soggy goats and their shelter,
Pulling down electric fences,
And tramping through the paddocks
Just made me feel alive.
My nose was runny and wet cool hairs streaked across my face.
My clunking gumboots even had a leak and a stone.
Yet
I had a smile in my heart.

115: Still Grey

A fortnight is a long time
To miss the sun.
Not so much the warmth.
Nor that its absence has brought incessant rain.
It is just the insipid grey
That drags your spirits down
To the bottom of your muddy shoes.

Maybe tomorrow,
As I'm opening my longing eyes,
Through my window
Will come
That welcome blue,
Herald of the sun.

But for now,
It is a conjured daydream
To cling to
And keep gloom at bay.
For still,
It is grey.

116: Newton's Third and Aspergers

Like Newton's third law,
For periods of excessive socialisation,
There must be periods of solitude.
For periods of stimulation and activity,
Periods of rest.
For periods where your responsibilities are for the welfare of others,
Periods dedicated exclusively to your own special interests.
To not adhere to the law
Will result in physical and emotional chaos,
Characterised by meltdown or shutdown.

Quite simple really!

117: Small Hauntings

There are fragments of memory that come back and bite.
They are just a flash,
Could be a whiff of fragrance, a gesture or a half-forgotten song,
But they have tendrils that drag you right back
To the moments when you can feel
That part of your heart
That is tender and unhealed.
The scar will not, quite, close over.

I call these moments ghosts.
For when they visit,
A coldness washes over me,
And I know that I am haunted.

Yet as time passes,
Ghosts become bored.
Your life fills with other responsibilities and distractions.
And your visitations decline.
And you are close to happy again.

119: The Stick

As I drive down the hill towards town,
The river attracts my attention.
No matter the conglomeration of thoughts,
Mercantile or familial,
Their colour or mood, filling my mind,
The slow pace of the water,
The harmonising rhythm of the overhanging willows,
Seduces my eyes.
I am drawn to dreaming of boating down its course
And picnicking on the sandbar on a curving bend.
We are now parallel and I am rising to a panoramic view.
Ahead in the distance there is a fisherman in waders.
He is in the water, close to the bank.
Closer inspection as we approach reveals
The same stick
Whose image has tricked my brain tens of times.

120: Abuse

It can be so subtle,
And the outside observer may not pick it.
They see the charm, politeness,
And nothing is too much trouble.
The trying too hard,
Immodestly feigning modesty,
All hallmarks of insecurity,
So easily overlooked.
The lovely family,
And such a nice guy.
His kids seem a little shy though.

But then there is the fuse,
So short.
The sudden blast,
When the pressure of the performance,
And the lack of power to completely control the situation,
Is too much.
And over such a little thing.
Speculate what may happen when the 'thing'
Is not so little.

123: Navigating

Life is filled with them,
Relationships through which you must navigate,
Like a ship sailing between treacherous reefs.
The coral-laden rocks and sandbars
Have no means of interpreting the skipper's intentions,
Or his motivation.
They sit static, looking innocuous.
Yet little eddies may turn into whirlpools.
Storms with strong winds may rage.
Like an ignorant fool you are led to disaster.
It seems on very rare occasion,
You can drop anchor in a quiet harbour.

128: Shearers Have No Bums

It looks comical,
Four shearers stand in a row,
Each with a reclining sheep's hoof between his bottom cheeks.
Shearers are lithe and wiry.
They need their belts,
To hold up their trousers.
They have no problems touching their toes,
And when they are on the long blows,
They kneel like sprinters on their blocks.
Shearers work very hard.
During breaks they stretch out on the board
To unbend their bent backs.
Shearers have soft hands,
From the lanolin,
With prickles
From the thistles.
Shearers are pranksters.
They brand the roustabout
And shave off his eyebrow.
Shearers like country music,
Hank, Slim and Johnny,
And they like it
Loud!

129: Flossie

She must have looked so cute as a little kid
When she melted someone's heart.
But she grew.
And so did her angora coat,
Into soft, white ringlets.
Her friendliness was praised,
And bemoaned, when she climbed up to be petted.
She bleated, 'Hello!' 'Please feed me!' 'I'm bored!'
And 'What-about me?'
Occasionally she ate things that were wanted for other purposes.
Sometimes she got into places she was not welcome.
Eventually her owners had to move and she was passed on
From one reluctant relative to another.
And now with her coat overlong,
Her hooves and horns in need of care,
And her bottom far from respectable,
She has come to us.
And we shall call her Flossie.

131: Gradually the Evening Gathers In

The blue and grey of the day slowly darkens,
To accentuate the mountains,
That hold us in their gentle embrace.
Inside it is cosy-warm.
The dancing flames of the fire mesmerise.
Dinner's aroma is filling the room with invitation.
Liberated from my workday shoes,
My feet are enveloped in soft sheepskin.
I recline into my familiar lounge chair,
Watch the bath-clean children quietly play at my feet.
Their damp hair dishevelled,
The just-recognisable smell of toilet soap.
I pick up my guitar, pick out a new tune and hum to myself.

132: The 'Arse-end' of Driving

My backside and the upholstery of my car's driver's seat
Have an intimate relationship.
They spend hours in each other's company.
They move together with synchronicity
And have moulded to each other's needs.
Although sometimes arriving numb at our destination,
My bottom is relieved to fall into the relative softness
Of the seat's padding
On the return journey.
The comparisons made between wear and tear on the car,
The hundreds of thousands of kilometres registered
On the odometer,
Could similarly be made on wear and tear
On my sedentary bum.
I am sure that its flat spots and lack of tone
Could be attributed to this.
Perhaps my bottom requires a 400,000-kilometre service,
And I should take a long walking holiday.

137: Blanche and Maude

Today we are gathered together,
(around the kitchen table)
To celebrate the lives of Blanche and Maude,
Who gave their lives unconsciously,
For the betterment of our nutrition.
They were with us for only seven short months,
But they brought their inquisitive and friendly dispositions
Into our lives to delight us.
Twice daily we met with them in their modest home
To provide their succour.
It was a pleasure to discover their individual personalities,
Watch them frolic and gamble about,
Happy in their sorority.
Their gentle and individual expressions, characteristic squeals
And exclamations of delight
Will remain etched in our memory.
They spent their final days romping in tall grass and playing together.
And fittingly, that is also how they left this world,
Together.
We have been honoured to have had the opportunity to raise
These magnificent pigs.

139: Cold

It creeps up slowly,
Engulfing by stealth.
Draw the coverings.
Pull it all in tight.
Each tiny gap a possible entry point.
Yet even when you are feeling secure,
Like chronic disease it gradually takes you over.
Until you recognise
That the chill is
Down to the bone.

142: Meltdown

Insidious how the stress creeps up.
Bubbling and gurgling just below the surface.
A look, an ill-timed word, a mistake,
Will bring the emotions bubbling to your eyes.
You can't always put your finger on the cause.
There are always the warning signs,
The rumbling.
You are impatient and snappy.
Small things irritate you.

Sometimes you can empty out a little of the stress,
By doing something you love.
Sometimes you can't.
And despite all your attempts to calm down,
Find your sanctuary.
Make sense of all the emotions.
One small thing will overfill that bucket
And you blow.

And sometimes there are casualties,
Those inadvertently caught in the crossfire.
And when everything calms down,
You are left to deal with the aftermath,
The shame,
And the knowledge that it will inevitably happen again.

143: Warm Water

The pressure of fluid against flesh,
Like an all-encompassing embrace
That demands nothing.
Float.
Escape the wear and tear of gravity on joints.
Hair slick and free from bondage.
No clothes to imprison
Or harness breasts.
Bare as if in the womb.
A warm bath is like a homecoming.

144: Ants In Their Pants

They have:
Ants in their pants.
A fascination with the contents of their nose.
A strong desire to pull a loose thread from the T-shirt nearest them.
An uncontrollable urge to scratch off the scab on their knee,
And eat it.
To put the corner of their worksheet into their mouth,
And chew off tiny pieces like a mouse.
To suck their sock.
To rock back.
To rock forwards,
And back again.
To chew their sleeve, shoelace,
The end of their pencil,
And their own hair.
To roll around the floor,
Or flip periodically onto their tummies.
An innate desire to fiddle
With something (whatever's in reach.)

Children of six or seven:
Bless them.

149: Sleeping On a Mountain Top

The climb was hard,
Leg-numbing, chest-burning, hard.
And all-the-more dangerous
For being executed in moonlight.
Although like midnight, the top would inevitably arrive,
It was a most longed-for object.
The promise of rest was all that guaranteed progress.
The stops became more frequent and the rocky inclines
More treacherous and steep.
At last it was achieved,
And among the rocks, on uneven ground,
The tent was erected.
Sweat-soaked body became chilled
And gratefully accepted the warmth of the sleeping bag.
Despite the chill and the rocky bedfellows,
Sleep was as unpolluted as the fresh crystal air of the clear night.
Unmolested by any discordant cacophony of thoughts.
Perhaps being physically closer to heaven
Sets the mind above the incessant buzz.

153: Opportunist

The table is easily accessed
If a chair is nearby.
All the delectable appetisers carefully arranged,
Each on its own plate.
The aromas tease and tempt,
Seductively stinging the nostrils with an aroma
That tantalises the palate.
The clear fluid of anticipation
Flows into the mouth.
Hesitation.
She knows it is forbidden,
And the consequences,
If she is discovered.
Yet she will descend to her base instincts
And make that illicit climb.
Chihuahuas are just like that.

161: My Bath – My Office

Despite also containing our home's only toilet,
The bathroom does not make such a bad office.
It is relatively private,
And the warm water and relaxed attitude to attire is a definite plus.
Being able to recline while tapping away on an iPad,
Or making necessary business phone calls is superior
To any ergonomic office chair.
My bath easily holds two,
So there is room for my secretary.
When the water gets cooler,
I can just let a little out of the plughole
And top it up with lovely hot water.
This is only disadvantageous when you are speaking on the phone.
I sometimes wonder at the thoughts of
A business contact on the other end
When they hear the echoing hollowness of this chamber,
Or the splash when I drop the soap.

162: The Clearing Sale

They're usually deceased estates,
A person's life placed out on black plastic,
Neat rows of furniture and household goods,
Room by room, like with like.
Picked apart like carrion.

Then the contents of farm sheds
And detritus from distant paddocks is brought together.
The new, the old and the in need of repair.
The farmers open trunks, lift bonnets and scratch their heads.

At ten o'clock the bidding commences.
There is a jocular attitude amongst those competing for bargains.
The auctioneer maintains a familial banter.
He puts a shiny gloss on the items, that only he can see.

I came for an old wool table.
Too small for a 'real' shearing shed.
But as I have only a handful of fleeces and my shed is small,
It was perfect.

The table is rickety, rugged and homemade.
The slats are young wattles.
And I love the honesty of its construction,
Born of necessity in a simpler time.
A covering of lanolin it wears like a badge of honour.

The mental image of this tool
Being used in my shearing shed,
Is a practical, romantic ideal
Too short-lived.
I could not outbid the fashionable lady from the city,
With the desire for a quaint pot plant holder.

164: Time to Think

Grant me time to think
When all those small burdens that sat
Quietly on my shoulders
Have flown like butterflies out into the expanse of the world.

Grant me a space in nature to sit
Where there are no distractions,
Or any ugliness to impede my view of this beautiful world.

Grant me comfortable weather
With no tempests or extremes of temperature
That restrict my opportunity to be outside,
To rejoice in solidarity with all things in my environment.

Grant me the companionship of a friend
Who can sit quietly with me in communion
And share with me this perfect moment in this time and this place.

171: The Salve

It is the paucity and precision,
Imagery and metaphor,
The musicality and lyricism,
Honesty and sentiment,
The mindful persistence,
Of well crafted, thought-provoking words
That make a poem
A salve to the soul.

172: Machismo

When they herd,
They butt up against each other
In mock jest,
Each sizing the others up.
They stand tall, legs apart and arms across chests,
A male mountain range.
Then come the stories:
Humorous, often sexualised, laced with profanity,
And ninety per cent true.
The level of exaggeration
The measure of their insecurity.

174: Human Frailty

Each day new systems are created
To control our lives.
To work or volunteer,
We need to maintain accreditation.
We must continue our professional development,
Assess risk,
And report, report, report.
Collect data on irrelevant minutiae
That may not withstand statistical scrutiny.
We set up these monoliths of data
To keep us safe.
But despite the protocols and the training,
The systems means nothing.
The human ego cannot stand the scrutiny.
It will not willingly reveal any fault or weakness.
Human beings lie or neglect to tell the truth.
All of these clever systems underestimate
Human frailty.

177: Aspie Life in a Medication Age

Life for a modern child is anything but simple.
No time now for lying in the sun gazing up at clouds
Or riding your bike around to a mate's house,
To see if they want to go swimming.
No billycarts,
Or cubbies in the bush on the vacant block next door.
No time or space
For solitude.

For Aspie kids, those were the halcyon days.
Well…compared to now.
Then you were just the odd, brainy kid who collected stuff,
And maybe talked in that weird voice.
You had the security of structure and certainty.
While you could be the plaything of the school bully,
So were other kids.

The bright blinking screens, ear-piercing squeals
Of fluorescent lights,
And stomach-churning, smelly whiteboard textas,
Were still to come.
The most distressing things then
Were competing in the school sports carnival,
The smell of Perkins paste,
And the sound of a teacher's fingernail
Inadvertently dragged across the blackboard.

People seemed to move slower.
Aspie kids did not have to resort
To escaping into their cyber worlds.
They could always hide away with the Famous Five,
In an adventure story, behind the weather shed.

But now if our Aspie kids are to be out
In this modern hurly burly,
Being overloaded by the very things that provide them solace,
It seems that medication is their only ticket to acceptance.

182: Asperger's

You do not grow out of Asperger's when you are twelve.
You learn to live in society the best you can.
Your unconventional behaviour and ambivalence
Are not due to poor parenting.
No newfangled diet will cure you,
Though a healthy diet is always beneficial.
Time and space for solitude and special interests
Is a must for everyone's sanity.
You are not androgynous or unsexual,
Just tactile – defensive, clumsy and super-sensitive.
You are also focused, passionate
And, most importantly, honest.

184: Simone de Beauvoir

Simone and Jean-Paul,
What a pair.
Experiments in love,
Open relationships,
Personal freedom and rights,
But responsibility…
Where?

Well, not to those third parties,
Broken-hearted,
Or swinging from a rope.
Love is not an experiment,
It is the overwhelming need
To share your life, your dreams…
Your hopes.

To trust another human being,
And without fear
Be yourself,
Them themselves.
And hold them…
Most dear.

And being with them is
Infinitely better
Than being without them.

186: Sewing Lesson

She wanted to learn.
I got out the old Brother.
First she learned how to drive on paper.
Her trepidation at pressing the pedal
Was palpable.
Where to put her fingers?
Then…
Clickity, clickety, stop.
Clickety, clickety, clickety, clickety stop.
She found her rhythm.
Onto reversing,
Then turning corners.
I think filling bobbins and threading the machine
Remain my domain,
At least for now.
Practising on actual fabric gave her confidence,
But sewing up her first drawstring bag,
I could see in her shining face,
Gave her satisfaction.

189: Morris on Gay Marriage

He is eight.
A ponderous deep thinker,
With impressive deductive powers.
And memory.
Morris is articulately blunt,
Providing intelligent commentary on his observations.
A rationalist.
Morris likes
Reading.
Morris dislikes
Anything scary.
Lately Morris has been quoting
'The Man from Snowy River,'
Extracts from *How to Train a Dragon*,
The Big Bang Theory and
the *Minion* movie trailer.
After listening to another comment about
Gay marriage,
Morris observes,
'Minions must have gay marriage,
Because they are all boys.'

190: Catharsis of Truth

The gnawing at the soul,
The heaviness carried in the chest,
The horrible nausea which drives the bile of unspoken words
Into gagging throats,
The unbearable strain on every joint,
As the burden of the bitter-tasting poison
Which flows
Like a sepsis through blood,
And fouls entire bodies,
Entire nations,
All this
Dissipates entirely,
And is lost within the realm of distant memory
When people are given the opportunity to
Speak their truth
And be acknowledged.

196: The Call of Wild Things

Too long in this stupor,
The relative shelter of brick and board,
Despite the windows,
Is stifling me.
Lethargy and malaise overpowers.
The grey hangs low and heavy,
Chills to the core of my soul.

I dream…
Wind lifting my hair and flushing my cool cheeks.
Soil and stone find temporary union with the mobile flesh
Of these bare soles.
Cool wet fronds slick against legs and squelch between toes.
Sunlight bathes my skin in a smiling warmth.
The music of creatures mingles with the soft percussion
Of water on pebbles.
Breathing deeply, crisp air cleanses my constrained lungs,
They inflate.
Around me I see the magnificent ordered disorder of nature.
And I run into this ecstasy.

197: The Flip Side of Adrenalin

Fight or flight?
Freeze into a vice-like grip.
Fighting words come fast and thick and slice like hot knives.
Cutting deep.
You will not surrender
Until all that pains you is ameliorated.
Yet you cannot see the way.
The casualties of battle become too great.
Many cowardly acts committed.
The shame unbearable.
The power cannot be maintained.
Will dissipates,
Battles cease.
The war postponed.
Adrenalin keeps the fighting spirit alive.
But at what cost?
Spirit broken, body bruised,
And the terrible weight of fatigue grinds you down
Into the ground.

203: Damaged Goods

I watched him physically and mentally deflate.
I had uttered words,
Not harsh or cruel but critical enough to overfill
His heavy bowl of hurt.

He receded into himself like a rose,
Deprived of sunshine – closing up.
Drooping from want of sustenance – lacking tenderness.

I watched the inner battle
With his mental demons,
Anxiety, fear, hopelessness.
Too strong and demanding,
Too great a foe to be vanquished
By one so young.

He put up a valiant fight.
I saw glimpses of his resolve
To fight down those tears.
They managed only to glaze,
His large round childish eyes.

So unfair
That a sweet babe must shoulder the weight
Of a bowl so full.
I feel my heartstrings straining at the terrible realisation
That I added to his burden.

205: Joy

From the time
We first emerge into the light
At birth,
Until the time
We lose that final battle
Against the dying of the light,
There is but one real goal:
The pursuit of joy.

207: Beards

It seems all the hipsters are growing
Luxurious beards.
My hubby,
Too lazy to shave for thirty years.
Has decided perhaps
A Santa-coloured beard
Is a premature accessory.
So now to shave,
And reveal his boyish complexion.
But to shave every day?

So he doesn't.
Kisses have become a graze hazard.
Gone the smooth softness of his bearded face.
Replaced by eighty-grit
Sandpaper!
I try hard,
Very hard,
To remain impartial and not influence him.

Just when it seemed
I would sport my own facial carpet rash…
Thank goodness,
He just couldn't get into the swing.
And has ceased shaving.
And for a change
Followed the cool set.

211: Partnership

Despite our differences,
We remain attracted.
And interested.
Interested enough to bother quarrelling.
Not settling for less
Than the best we can get from each other.
Yet at times communication breaks down.
Each falls into destructive patterns
That lose sight of the precious gift
Of loving somebody.

212: Disneyfied

Don't get me wrong,
I weep and giggle like the rest of the theatregoers,
Yet I despair
At the comprehension and vocabulary of my students
When it becomes impossible to share classic children's literature.
They can only cope with the happily ever after,
Sanitised, supersized, sassy,
Disrespectful, consumerist, fast-paced, product-placed
Versions of stories.
No thinking required.
And the baddy always gets their comeuppance.
Action every second.
Definitely no time for reflection.
Click and go gratification.
The little mermaid can't really sacrifice herself
For the happiness of her prince.
Not if she's a curvy redhead called Ariel.
Cinderella has blonde hair and a blue dress,
Didn't you know?
And of course Robin Hood is a fox.

213: The Solemnity and Reverence of Falling Snow

The slow procession of flakes,
Dropping daintily from the sky,
Like a choreographed ballet,
Fills me with a sacred awe.
The forest quietens
As the birds and animals
Speak in moderated tones.
Their home has become a light-filled cathedral
And they demonstrate respect for its majesty.
I become mesmerised by the passage of single flakes
And feel my soul cleansed and nourished
By the freshness of this pure modest spectacle.

214: The Off Switch

Two point two children.
'Oh we are going for the third – to try for a boy.'
'Couldn't possibly go through that again.'
'Even numbers, so we wanted four.'

I cried when my husband got a vasectomy.
I was forty-two and was on to number eight.
I know that the little switch that tells us
That we have now produced sufficient progeny
In my case is faulty.

I know I'm not alone.
I know elderly mothers who track down the new mothers
In the supermarket,
Just to have that fix of newborn baby smell.
I watch them absentmindedly ruffle the head of a passing toddler.

We recognise each other.
Those women and I.
We know that when we are sitting gaga in the nursing home
We will be the ones grasping a baby doll to our flabby breasts.

216: Delayed Gratification

I mourn for the loss of delayed gratification.
When life was simple and choices few,
When waiting for the next ball or picnic races
Was exciting.
But we can no longer wait and we needn't.
Our pace increases with the loss of each local service.
No longer doing the weekly shop in the local village,
Time is spent travelling the hundreds of kilometres
To the doctor, dentist, even the supermarket.
Local sport, entertainment gone.
Wait for the next blockbuster movie to wend its way to the bush?
Download and watch,
Right now.
My back has moulded into the form
Of my car's driver's seat.
I have a closer relationship with that than my hiking boots.
It seems these devourers of time
Give us less opportunity to enjoy
The rapture of anticipation.

219: Strained Relations

We go through the motions of civility.
The elephant looks on.
She is wearing a bright pink tutu
With silver spangles.
She (the elephant)
Knows it looks ridiculous.
But how else does she get our attention?
Despite all her attempts,
Pulling faces, blowing raspberries and calling our names,
Neither of us will stray from the script.
We smile and make banal small talk.
I feel my stomach squeeze into a tighter ball.
The meeting ends.
I put my hand on the elephant's shoulder reassuringly.
Maybe next time we'll ditch the fancy dress.

221: Made by Hand

My son is dismissive.
'Why waste your time?
You can pick up slippers at Aldi.
You're just povo.'
But I'm not.
Poverty is not seeing the workmanship,
The care and love,
That went into his little brother's moccasins.
A goat pelt I tanned,
From a kid I raised,
That fed our family.
The little foot I measured,
And the leather I softened and stitched.
Little brother was out playing
With his headband of cockatoo feathers,
His wattle bow and arrow.
The timing was serendipitous.
He loved his new slippers,
Genuine
Moccasins.

225: Sanctuary

My sanctuary will be comfortable.
There will be no expectations,
And no responsibilities.
Anything I want to create
Will be at my fingertips.
When I want company it will be there.
When I want solitude,
No one will disturb me.
The radio will be on,
And the presenter will have
The soothing voice of Michael Cathcart
Or the late Alan Saunders,
And they will only discuss interesting topics.
I will not suffer from any apprehensions,
Knowing that I am free to enjoy the sanctuary,
Indefinitely.

228: Resolution

Despite my meltdown,
Sometimes only an action from me
Will break the stalemate.
The time goes on too long,
The distress too great.
The rescuer requires rescuing.
Even when things seem hopeless,
There can be a brief moment
When a small crack
Lets in a splinter of light.
I seize the opportunity
With two hands,
Rip the grey sky apart
To let in the light.
Feel the warm sun on my face.
Reach for your hand and we go out in it,
Together.

232: Blue versus Grey

It was two things,
The blueness
Between billowing clouds
That slowly sailed across the sky,
And the warmth of the sunshine
That kissed the bare skin of my face and hands.
It was these
That lifted every aspect of my being.

The soft dry ground on which I lay
And the caressing breeze
That played like a lover with my unfastened hair
Added to the effect.
I could smell the familiarity of frost-seared grass
And hear the country sounds
Of those on hoof, paw and wing.
And I felt calm.

But all too soon,
Despite the patches of blue,
The sun's warming rays were taken prisoner
By a cold grey cloud.
I was suddenly frozen to the core.
My idyll broken,
I went inside
To the warmth of the fire.

233: Sometimes You Just Stop

It creeps up slowly.
It is not exactly a malaise.
Your spirit remains intact.
You are not feeling hopeless or despairing.
Yet you are simply
Not feeling.

But as you must
Do something,
You do what is closest to hand.
Write these observations
Into poetry.

Sit, not comfortably,
On the hearth rug,
Your outside coat
Still on.
Your outside shoes also
Still on.
Ignore the twinges of pain your back,
And the pins and needles in your feet.
The fire's warmth compensates.

You have one focus,
The task at hand.
He has made you a cup of tea,
But you have insufficient will
To move your hand to take it up.
Now he has asked you a question.
But you can't think,
To make any decision.

This is what it is like when you are full.
Detached!

235: The Wombat

Today we sent a wombat to heaven.
He stumbled blindly in the harsh daylight.
His nocturnal clock out of whack.
This a clear sign.
The scourge?
Mange from a now fox-less burrow.

I have been guilty of verbally abusing wombats.
They make night drives a heart-stopping event.
Their choice of home often inconvenient,
And their aerial ablutions on farm equipment irritating.
(How can such a stubby-legged animal defecate at such heights?)

Suburbanites have no idea of the challenges of wombats.
Yet when you are surprised by one out grazing at night,
Its jaunty jog, digging and snuffling about are endearing.
Supine baby wombats with their soft leathery pads
And chubby bellies melt your heart.

Today was this wombat's last day.
He was huge and powerful,
But so fragile.
Bothered by our yapping foxie,
He barely moved away.
His thick winter coat encrusted and scabby.
We would not let him suffer the indignity of a slow death.
Damn mangy foxes.

239: The Gang

Contrast flashes, white against black,
Moving up into the trees
In organised mayhem.
These are a young gang of hoodlums.
This is their patch.
My approaching car precipitates
A flight for cover.
Their numbers have grown,
A few more recruits have joined.
It is a welcome to spring sight.
The coolest gang of white-winged choughs
On the block.

240: Third

They do go in threes,
The matriarch, the retired farmer and now the mechanic.
I was secretly hoping that he wouldn't make the trifecta.
But he went at last.

When I was twenty-two,
Young, eager
And naïve,
I felt his gruff exterior abrade.
But I did not know his humour then.

I have been travelling the vital years of my life,
Marriage, children, maturity.
And he has been a constant,
Smiling knowingly
Each time my car met with an unexpected mishap.
'You do realise that these things need oil.'

A Catholic, dad seven times,
He fuelled my car and enjoyed my kids,
Tapping at the glass, smiling or engaging them in chat.

He told me once that he had raised those garage doors
Every working day of his life since he was fourteen.
His son, third generation, has recently updated them.
No need to put on the gloves and pull hard on the chain,
The new blue doors roll up easily.

In hindsight,
It seems an unfortunate omen.

242: Optimism of a Sunny Day

Potential
Not yet realised but…
In your mind's eye you can see it.
You dampen down the doubts,
Tramp them with possible contingencies.
It seems to be the sunshine,
After an extended period of grey,
That brings on the dreams.

244: Of This Town

He was of this town
From the moment his eyes first perceived light
Till they closed, as his light went out.
As he sat in the hospital in the next town,
His thoughts were always of his return.
The Catholic church on the hill,
The house of his childhood,
The garage,
The town's water supply tank.
The pump house,
The golf club,
And his marital home,
These were the boundaries
Of his life.
Within this town,
He grew, was educated, loved and was loved.
Here he found and served his community.
Here he was often happy.
Perhaps in the grand scheme of things,
Many may not find it worth celebrating,
Yet it was still a remarkable life.

247: Ski Resorts

Perhaps it was my Aspie dislike of crowds.
Perhaps the glossiness of the thin facades.
Maybe the faux Europe style of architecture that grated.
The wankiness of the beverages and confectionery on sale.
I could not put my finger on it,
The discomfort I felt,
When we arrived at the resort.

I enjoyed the drive, despite the heavy traffic.
The uniqueness of snowgum woodland, snow-covered,
The rounded rocks and herbage of the fast-flowing crystal creeks.
I was especially drawn to those.
The air too and the snow-deadened quiet.
The company was good and tobogganing promised to be fun.
Yet…

The resort was a Formica table in a Georgian mansion.
The surface cleaned to such a sheen that the reflected light
Blinded me.
No trees, just snow and bitumen.
The beautiful people were pretentious and orchestrated.
The uncool wannabes tried too hard, used far too much peroxide,
Squeezed bulgy bodies into unflattering snowsuits,
And wore excessive putty-like make-up.
Families with screaming toddlers,
Tortured by freezing hands,
Made half-smiles and took multitudes of photos,
Proof that they were affluent enough to be here
And were having fun (sic).

248: The Hottie

Dear Lord,
I give thanks on this cool evening
For the simple practicality
Of my hot-water bottle.
For the manufacturers, distributors,
And the small grocery store proprietors,
Who made it possible for me to procure one.
Also to the thoughtful friend who sewed a cover for said hottie
And gave it as a birthday present to my husband,
Who also in kindness, knowing my chilly disposition,
Passed it onto me.
May they, and particularly my husband,
Who nightly fills it with hot water,
When he brings me an Earl Grey in bed,
Feel the warmth of my blessings,
As I feel the warmth of my hottie.

Amen

249: Changing Tack

When people get into a rut,
It is a euphemism
For getting stuck in some humdrum routine.
Those with Asperger's also get into ruts,
Though not anything necessarily humdrum,
But it may sometimes be routine.
We etch a rill into our minds,
Through excessive focus.
We put almost our whole being
Into some of the things we do.
This is the key to our successes.
This is also our undoing.

Our focus excludes.
We appear aloof and uncaring.
But in actuality,
We are not ambivalent,
Just oblivious.
And when the world external to our focus point
Blares at us and demands our attention,
The shock is physical.
It jars.
We slowly recover and submit.
But the rut is very deep.
It takes time to change tack.

251: Chris the Sheep

Lamb of the Monaro,
Beneath the stark blue sky,
In the frost hollows, tree line inverted,
Chris the Merino grew to wetherhood.
Spurned by his shorn brethren,
And frightened by men and their stockyards,
He fled.
At first his growing coat was a comfortable barrier
To winter gales, rain, sleet and occasional snow.
In summer he sought the cooler shelter of the wooded hills.
Time passed but his overgrown staple
Continued to overgrow.
He became dwarfed by his prison of fleece.
As he passed from lamb to two-tooth to old mutton,
His burden only became greater.
By sheer luck he remained upright.
Many a less-laden sheep has turned turtle and perished,
With ridiculous legs gesticulating to the heavens.
Luck was on his side.
For he was spotted
After six years of avoiding the board,
And with great fanfare,
Shorn.
Chris the sheep,
Cultivator of the heaviest fleece
In the history of shearing.

254: Homes for under 100k

Apparently Australia's population has ballooned
To twenty-four million.
But they don't live here.
Our heyday has been fed out to the sheep and cattle,
By ageing farmers.
Our preschool is now a pile of unused toys in the corner
Of three local halls.
Doctor?
He is accumulating hours for his pilot's licence,
As he comes flying up from the coast.
Our lone policeman,
He of the state's largest beat,
Can't go to the post office without his bullet-proof vest
Because it is also the pub.
He drives in his 4WD festooned with aerials,
But can't attend an incident
Without back-up from two hours away.
Two families announce that they are leaving the area,
The school will have to make some drastic readjustments,
(and who knows what ramifications they will have.}
The specialty shop fronts even in the larger towns are emptying.
How long will the local independent grocer hang on
When the punters will go to Aldi on their next doctor's visit?
(People don't get sick in time for the once-a-month flying visit.)
But the place is gorgeous.
The air and water are clean.
There is room to move,
And think…

And there are homes for sale for less than a hundred k.

259: The Fragility of the Human Ego

Frustrated tone of voice,
A sideways glance,
Some ill-phrased words,
A simple misunderstanding,
So little to unbalance the delicate mechanism.
Retorts and recriminations,
Amplification and divisive speech,
All facilitate the formation
Of gangs and factions,
Busy isolating and excluding.
Their status quo and standing are retained.
As the tall poppies are cut down
By lesser creatures,
Those on the edge watch on and ponder
The purpose of it all.

260: Some Compartments of my Life

I live my life within smallish compartments of time,
Each with its individual focus
To which I give my fullest attention.

The compartment of writing this poem,
Contains the fantastical images
That make metaphors
And give me the words.
I let them out to play upon the page,
And make music in my ears.
These thoughts make me smile inwardly.

The compartment of sharing my thoughts and ideas
With another human being,
Feeling the welcomeness of their company,
The sound of their unique voice,
The warmth of their presence,
And familiarity of their smell,
The solidarity of being so joined in his moment,
Makes my heart swell in the cavity of my chest.

The compartment of remembered moments.
This is where I recollect, I sit quietly,
And reflect upon recent happenings.
The times when I felt connected and comfortable.
The moments that fortified my heart with joy
And of those individuals to whom I am connected.
This makes my soul sing and ache at the same time
As I miss them.

261: The Aftermath

After the journey into the cauldron of sensory stimulation
Comes the aftermath.
Bowl filled with the conviviality of relationships.
Bowl filled with the angst of unmet expectations
Bowl filled with the pain of fragile egos bruised.
Bowl filled with the joy of new possibilities.

I return to more familiar territory,
The contents of my bowl are tossed and stirred.
Relive the petty conflicts and strategise their resolution.
Relive the disappointments and plan for a better outcome
Next time.
Relive the joyful, invigorating comfort of close relations
And pang for the loss of their intimacy.
Rest, joy and some resolution may slowly drain my overfull bowl.

262: The Grazier's House

The grazier's grand home was at the wrong end of the bush track.
His children had moved on to more lucrative pursuits.
The wool stockpile fell on the price guarantee,
And Australia fell off the sheep's back.

The grazier was old, and needed a beach bungalow.
Or at least his wife did.
Or perhaps she just wanted the shops,
And access to hairdressers that coastal resort towns afford.
It was her turn.

The grazier shuffles behind his wife on auto-pilot,
The walking dead in shining RM Williams.
The grazier's property is under pine.
Generations of blood and tears lie buried beneath
The acidifying, needle-strewn soil.
And there too lies the grazier's heart.
Best he does not see what his grand home has become.

263: The Benefits of Solitude

He said, 'You should go.'
So I did,
Cast off responsibility,
The things that could now wait
Just a few more hours.
And I drove
To almost the end.
The way was rough,
I felt some trepidation,
But also invigoration,
Because of the risk.
Then I left the relative protection
Of my big, strong modern car
And walked.
The air was alive with the song of insects and birds,
Fleet-footed wallabies startled me.
The breeze played upon my cheeks
And the sun danced in my eyes.
The blue removed the grey within my soul
And the rapid beating of my heart,
Reminded me that I am alive.
Conversations and scenes played in my mind.
Bad feelings were removed
And I felt the natural world hold me in its embrace.

269: Billie-Grace Car Washing Service

Her big blue eyes, that are mine,
Look at me through the windscreen.
On the bonnet, her five-year-old hands are rubbing at the glass.
She has a damp nappy that was once hers.
I feign sleep so I can observe her without further engagement.
She is busy,
Making small smearing circles.
Her hard work is not effective
Yet she persists.
Her tongue pushes about her mouth in the same circles.
She is concentrating hard.
As she returns the washcloth to the bucket.
I watch her lips form the shape of a song.
She is singing while she works.

272: The Tough Nut

'I go to bed when I want.
Two-thirty sometimes.
I can watch whatever telly or DVDs I want,
Mum and Dad don't fuck'n' care.
Yeh, I just do what I like.
So you can't make me…'

He is short and stocky.
Rosy round cheeks match
His little round belly.
He looks tough,
But his face is lost
So easily.
Don't challenge him, he'll break.

He is a grimy cherub,
With a foul mouth.

275: The Buzz

He said,
'You were buzzing last night.
I could feel you vibrating.'
I knew what he was talking about.
The atoms of my body had been thrust
Through thousands of kilometres,
At a hundred kilometres an hour,
Driving.
The tyres of my car dragged against the bitumen,
Their vibration travelled through my seat,
Into spine and the marrow of each of my bones.
The cochlea of my ears endured the hours of banshee screaming,
Of air scraping against the car's exterior,
As high-pitched as a fluorescent light.
Drone, drone, drone,
Ever rhythmic, the motor's base,
Coming into my feet on the floor,
And my hands on the steering wheel.
I had been a human tuning fork.
And now, free from vehicular prison,
I rang out.

276: Nature Girl

She does not speak with her mouth,
My Rett's girl.
Her eyes and sparkling smile tell me of her love.
For the sun and its optimistic warmth,
It kisses her face and dazzles her seeking eyes.
For the wind and its merry dance amongst the limbs of the tree.
It whips hair into her blinking eyes and smiling mouth.
Of birds calling from all corners and out of view.
They flit about branchlets of the tree carrying nesting,
Of leaves and their soothing rustle.
They mimic her sparkle as they flutter,
Showing alternately their front and back.

I sit and watch as she absorbs her environment,
And receives grateful succour from it.

279: The Songwriter

I am learning his song.
Recorded in a hospice.
He was a songwriter.
Which really means
He was a poet.
I could see him in his lyrics.
I could feel his pain, his optimism,
And the love he had for his wife.
I could feel his gratitude,
For the opportunity to reveal himself
So publicly.
No truer portrait
Than this self-portrait.
Each time I tried to sing it…

The poignancy of the last line
Caught in my throat.

280: Pissing in his Pocket

It was just so apt.
Looking in from the outside.
The way was clear,
To me at least.
All these people getting soooo upset,
And over nothing.
Were they blind, stupid?
Apparently.
But it was simple really.
All I had to do to remedy the intractable situation
And get the immovable moving
Was…
'Piss in the right pocket!'

282: He's Crying

My infants class are restless on the carpet.
The maths lesson is going longer than their concentration span.
They fidget.
One picks furtively at the books on the shelf,
One has their socks in their mouth.
I know that it is time to wind it up,
Before the learning moment is lost.
Then it is his turn.
The child with too much going on at home.

His wide smile and over-eagerness show
That he is excited to be up next.
But he has not understood the question.
Before my eyes I watch him crumple.
His eyes look shocked and bewildered.
Everything droops like a flower deprived of rain.
Tears well in his eyes.

And I explain that it is all right.
(I want to hold him, but of course I can't.)
'We only learn from our mistakes,' I say.
He tries to explain his confusion,
But he can't.
His eyes are leaking now,
And the other kids are ready to cut him, the weakest, down.
They have the blood lust.
I must save his face.
'Stop!'

All eyes are on me.
I have their attention.
I apologise for not phrasing the question better.
'It is just a misunderstanding.
I have confidence that you will get this perfectly right
Now you understand,' I say.
And he does.
'Sometimes we just can't choose when we will cry,' I say.

Our philosophical discussion goes till lunchtime.

285: The Scouts and the Witches

Unlikely cohabitants,
We Scouts and the witches.
Yet we are both tribes,
Our uniform and coded language attest.
While they make merry with mead,
We have red and white wine at our formal dinner.
They, their athanes, garlands and flowing gowns,
We have scarves and woggles.
They will dance around the maypole,
(Perhaps sky-clad),
Our eyes upcast salute the flagpole.
They welcome the coming of spring,
We await jamboree.
What make they of our raucous BRAVOs?
We are definitely apprehensive about their 'great rite'
As we retire to our segregated bunk rooms.
Blessed be!

286: The Wave

Last night when we made love,
It happened again.
I tried so hard to remain grounded.
To stay with you in those moments.
But I felt them moving in me.
Coming from that well, deep inside.
They bubbled up very quickly,
And I was caught unguarded.

Every uncomfortable discourse,
Each uncertain social interaction.
The crash, clatter, whirr and constant drone
Of this adulterated, wonderful world,
Every miscue and faux pas,
The rolled eyes and the cringes,
The joy and excitement,
All the stresses,
And the exuberance of just being me.
In those moments I felt them flow up and out.
A bottle effervescing with emotion.
More than I could handle.
I lost sight of you,
And was left to ride this wave,
Alone.

287: Don't Settle for Less

Out there in the wide wide world,
There is someone
Who lives with the exuberance to match your passion.
Who likes to run and climb and hike up mountains
And lie on quiet hilltops to gaze at the stars.
Who will suddenly see you,
And unbidden bound into your arms.
Will match your caresses with their own.
Whose sweet voice will be like soft silk on your eardrums
And whose every recess will match your curves,
So that you will fit together like Lego.
They will smell just right,
And will thrust their face deep into your nape
And take in long draughts
Of essence of you.
They will be your complement.
And you will regret any time that you missed
Before you met.

290: I Should be Sleeping

Sleep.
It is very underrated,
Yet so welcome,
When the undertow of fatigue,
Pulls at all your vitals,
And drags you down,
Into deep unconsciousness.

I know I should submit.
In my rational mind.
Yet it is my rational mind that prevents me.
Too many interesting thoughts.
Too large a sensory meal to digest.

Oh grant me a firm, warm bed,
Sunny, breeze-dried sheets,
Well fitted,
A plump pillow,
And you,
To entwine with my legs.

Then perhaps I should sleep.

292: In Bed in the Afternoon

It is delightfully decadent to be lounging in bed
In the afternoon.
Five unsupervised
But I can hear their voices,
Occupied in various levels of activity.
The cluck and clatter of scooters on concrete.
Rhythmic as they clear each expansion joint.
In the kitchen, banana smoothies are in production
And the blender whirrs.
No doubt at least one will be curled up with a book.
But I am warm and the pillow welcomes my heavy head.
My naked skin too, the comfort of soft cotton against it.
There will be consequences for retreating like this.
But right now,
It is the weight of my weary body resting in this comfortable nest,
That is my primary focus.

294: My Tribe

My tribe are misunderstood.
On the edges looking in.
We are honest as the day is long,
Loyal to our ideas, ideals and our friends.
Happy to plough our own furrow most of the time.
Have sensory super powers.
Are rational pragmatists.
Disoriented by the difference between what a person says verbally
And their body language.
Ignorant of pecking orders and social standing.
Are difficult to offend but easy to crush.
Are mono-focused and frequently oblivious.
Are passionate, empathetic and compassionate…
Just frequently ignorant to other's needs.
We require periods of solitude.
Are talented and intelligent.
Naive and easily taken advantage of,
We are into purpose, not ego,
And find our busy, amazing, stimulating and wonderful world
Overwhelming sometimes.

295: The Reassurance of Hills

To be surrounded by forested mountains,
Is to be embraced in a hard, cool freshness,
Much like a firm hug
From a parent straight from an ocean swim.
It is comforting and invigorating.
Wet body – cold,
Smell – unpolluted, natural, familiar.

To run about on a grassy hilltop
Is to feel as free as flying.
Wind fills your hair and lungs,
It caresses your skin,
And the warm sun smiles
Down on your upturned face.

After driving for many hours on monotonous plains,
I look out for the hills on the horizon.
It seems that my soul requires
The reassurance of hills.

296: Time to Fish

The barometer is showing 'headache'.
The pressure is heading for storms
And the kids are fractious and whingey.
The afternoon is slowly cooling,
And an almost full moon is rising.
Looking out the window absentmindedly,
I could sense it before I saw the signs.
It is time
To stop all the pointless chores,
To go outside,
Grab that jar full of fresh-dug bush worms,
The rod and bag,
And go fishing.

The ants are flying.

297: Leave the Water on – An Ode to the Bathtub

Oh great receptacle of iron cast
That within its warmed contents,
I enjoy a sweet repast
Of solitude.

And at the day's end,
Wash away the bitter stresses,
And send
Them into purgatory.

For who could resist
The water's sweetest tinkling
As it kissed
The enamelled edge.

Or the velvet tenderness,
As it caressed my weary flesh.
For me, such feelings of happiness
As those
Are not so often expressed
In prose.

Yet my tub and I shall thus sojourn
Through pleasant evenings of our life.
Once I have left, and clothing donned,
Will yearn
To be within its soft embrace
Again.

299: To My Aspie Wife

Loving you has been easy. Living with you has been more difficult.
Years have been taken to smooth the edges of our misunderstandings.
I feel the passion of your embrace, the eagerness of your lips,
Casting power into a place of joy.
An abrasive word, a false smile, too much stimulation,
Spiral us into a maelstrom of harsh words and pain.
A gulf opens that only true words can bridge.

You are not from this world of lies and competitive social protocols.
Your star has an honest shine;
Its illumination direct to my soul,
No pretence or agenda blocks the clarity.

Real friends are openly rewarded,
An intensity of empathetic communication –
Crafting connections and glowing hearts,
You must beware the snide remark, the jealous put-down,
A closing of ranks against the stranger.

Alone in an isolated confusion of unfathomable rules,
Clashing body language and pecking orders.
Your spirit quashed, breath held till superseded
By solitude's relief or meltdown's curse.

I am part you, spooning into your body,
Thoughts flowing from the headlights of your intelligence,
Beautiful ideas staining me with colour,
Possibilities your life force –
Solutions no problem.

Sensitivities require consideration,
Meaningful language a negotiation,
Miscued pitfalls avoided,
Intimacy prioritised.
Constraints released to promote the vitality and necessity,
Of you being free, understood and grounded –
Connected to me.

300: Beltane Lost

Children carve pumpkins,
Kept in cool store.
It's Halloween in Australia.
Here the wheel of the year turns widdershins,
Out of sync.
And the old year dies six months prematurely.
The God of the tribe
Does not get to lay with his Land Goddess.
The only metaphorical orgasm
Is of mindless consumerism
That is the new religion.

301: Fledglings

Feather and claw grotesque,
Posture distorted,
Eye dulled,
The road is littered:
Australian raven, magpie and chough.
All struck before they knew
The ecstasy of flight.

306: The Date

Today we walked in nature.
Felt the strain of lungs and muscles
As we climbed.
Looked down into a cavernous ravine.
Watched fast-moving water swirl and boil over rocks,
And heard its cry.
Were scratched and bruised by vegetation.
Listened for the waterfall.
Climbed down the precipice tentatively.
Slid on scree.
Hopped from boulder to boulder.
And scrabbled.
Sat beneath a gum and ate a picnic.
Drank cool, unadulterated and dynamic water.
Shed our material skins and dived.
Felt the shock of sudden coolness.
Defied gravity and floated downstream.
Cleaned sand-clad feet, to put on socks.
Climbed again.
Wiped sweat from above our lips,
And felt it drizzle down our backs.
Saw smiles.

Felt the satisfaction of our own healthy bodies.
The perfect way to spend a day.

308: Shades of Love

I believe in shades of love.
The lighter shades
Are the love of nature, animals and humanity.
The pastel shades are love for your babies.
These grow to brighter colours as they mature
And become themselves.
And become a little more muted as they gain
Independence from you.
There are the passionate primary colours of attraction
And new love
That become more earthy and nature-based
As you make a life together.
There is the patchwork of friendships
In varying depths and hues.

All these shades of colour nourish and enrich you.
Within this kaleidoscope you live.

309: I Know I Love You Because I Miss You

It is not what you do,
How you look,
What you feel like,
How good a lover you are,
How compatible we are,
Or the interests we share.
It isn't even your conversation,
Or your unique smell.
It is not because my friends say we make a good couple,
Or that I am lucky to be with you.
It is not because we made children together,
Have shared assets.
It is most definitely not to avoid loneliness,
Or that I have made my bed and must now sleep in it.

The fact is that I know I love you
Because I am happier being with you
Than being without you.
I think conversations to you when we are apart.
And in those quieter moments,
When I am not distracted by other thoughts or responsibilities,
I miss you.

311: Being Moved

I was not moved by the loss, the despair,
The real and perceived dangers.
Not by the anguish of the victims or their families.

I was not moved by the speeches,
Of the people of consequence.
I was not moved by the warmongering
Of those seeking retribution and revenge.

No.

The courageous people
Who stood strong and did not give into hatred,
Who refused to be defined
By those who, because of their own suffering,
Chose to kill and maim their loved ones.

Those who refused to turn on their neighbours,
Who act out of love and compassion,
Despite their own unbearable suffering.

These are the people who move me to tears.

Vive.

315: On Dogs and Some Men

My new dog cowers.
He has 'submit' written on his forehead.
Even my mini-foxy can have him retreating,
Head and ears down,
Crouched,
Tail held stiffly between his legs.

He is my new dog
Because his owners,
Lovers of many dogs,
Knew that he was bottom of the pack.
The alpha male,
A tall border collie, was his constant torment.
He, as a young entire male,
Would not have any place in this pack.

The law of the jungle
Uses violence to maintain power.
But we humans are not dogs,
We can make better choices,
More humane choices.

My friend has a broken heart.
A broken spirit,
And her beautiful face is broken too.
In the pack,
At the party,
She found herself excluded.
She upset the alpha male,
Her boyfriend,
So his pack set on her.
Beat her and left her unconscious
On a suburban street.

Same law of the bully,
Just a different jungle.

319: The Daisies

The hill of feral daisies is in flower again,
I know they are a weed,
But beautiful in their bounty nonetheless.
They measure the springtimes,
Since I met you.
Despite the fact that we have parted.
You, like the daisies, are part of me.
And when I see them,
It is that summer,
All over again.
When I fresh-faced picked posies
To fill my small rented cottage.

I remember
How each year they slowly crept
Out from their stronghold,
The travelling stock reserve,
And down the road like each season's
Grazing cattle.
The cows and the cars
Have spread them almost to town.

The other afternoon,
As I was driving home,
I saw a patch on my own road.
The daisies are moving closer to me.
So I shall have an annual reminder
Near at hand.

320: The Subtleties of Misogyny

Misogynists are not always full of machismo.
Sometimes they are placid, misguided souls,
Protective,
And maybe self-characterised as
Gentlemen,
Even chivalrous.
No, they do no real harm –
So they think.

Yet their gender stereotypes are ingrained.
It is them,
To their very souls.

By their ineptitude they court
A well-meaning
Feminine guiding hand
Who soon becomes a dog's body.
Somehow we are duped
By their charming hopelessness.

They are aggrieved that their
Sensitive new age men's club
Should be perceived as
Unwelcome to female members.
Yet it is, by its old boy, back-scratching,
Laissez faire attitude,
Exclusive.

And heaven help
The immodestly loud and persistent woman
Who might challenge any one of them.
For she is a harridan.

321: Intimacy

Stay present with me as we negotiate
The uneven path that is our intimacy.
Look into my eyes
And tell me with those mirrors of your soul
Your darkest secrets and most private desires.
Speak the words that speak your truth.
Listen for mine.
Read my gestures.
Keep the bond unbroken.
Do not stray into
Your own secret places
But be with me
Until the cacophony
Of our everyday lives intrudes
And we must again part.

323: Shut Down

When all your systems shut down,
You cannot speak.
Yet in your head,
The conversation goes on.

They,
The ones who love you,
Ask questions
You cannot answer,
Will not answer,
Or are so upset
(Because they know you are mute,
But persist in the incessant ridiculous questioning,
And back you into a corner)
That you will EXPLODE
If you answer.

And then you will be ashamed
Because it is not their fault
That you are full.

324: And They Walked

There is no one untouched.
'I don't know how many laps I can do
But I'm walking for Carol.'
Carol is on morphine now.
A few weeks ago she was among the sopranos
In our community choir.
Penny and her sisters have raised so much.
Ignoring the signs.
Like a man,
Their dad succumbed after only a few short weeks.
As night falls,
The candles are silent sentinels.
Their scribbled messages
Each tell a story of loss
Or sometimes hope.
I walk for the collective loss.
Those of my friends.
Their sister, daughter, aunt.
His mate, a long way away.
I walk in gratitude of good health.
Relay for Life.

325: Broken

The brave face is a charade.
Quick step with resolve.
Dark sunglasses, tight jaw.
Not waiting for the change at the checkout.
Shaking hands, and trembling lip.
Three inches deep
Instant coffee shaken into her cup.
And a packet of cigarettes,
Burnt into smoke rings,
Go up her nose.

He has broken her.

326: She Just Didn't Love Him

She was surprised
That she was not heartbroken.
She expected to feel sad
That they had been torn apart.
She did not even miss him.

There had been good times.
And they had been together for a year.
And it was not that he had betrayed her,
And watched as she was beaten.
She was not bitter or vengeful,
Just confused.
She didn't care to ever see him again.

'Well, you just didn't love him,' I said.

'I suppose I didn't,' she replied.

330: Holding On

The trust has been dented.
And now I'm clinging, white-knuckled,
To the barricade
I built to protect me.

I am not yet giving in to the maelstrom of emotion
That will wash over me like a tsunami,
Toss me and leaving me gasping for air
When I do go back
To the relative safety of his embrace.

The hurt is great.
The return, slow and painful.
He, who was supposed to be my rock,
Crumbled into dust
Before my sadness.

I, in despair,
That he,
Who should,
Did not recognise me.
So I drove him away.

And now I am left,
Just holding on.

331: The Casual Affair

Why is it
He cannot allow himself to love her?
To give his whole self,
Openly and honestly.

Yet he longs for her caress,
Her lithe body against his,
And her voice in his ear,
Soft and low.

She will give,
And give, to her very soul,
Yet he does not trust.
He is honest when he tells her
That he cannot commit,
But she hopes he is lying.

For fear that he will be hurt,
He holds back,
And hurts them both.

335: The Swag

A marvellous invention,
Of antipodean origin,
Humped on the wallaby,
A non-complaining partner,
Who will let you lie as is your wont,
Keeping out cold and rain,
But allowing a vista unparalleled in beauty,
The majesty of heaven itself.

The subject of verse and song,
Or meandering yarn,
Told at leisure by a campfire.

When a long day of crutching,
Or mustering or marking lambs,
Fishin' or huntin',
Is at an end,
Or after a night partying too far from home,
This is the time
To find a soft flat piece of ground
(or the back of a ute)
And roll out
Your swag.

338: Humanity on Parade

Stuck in town.
Now I am a retail prisoner.
Before me the food court.
Saccharine smells
Blend with coffee and grease.
I scan looking for the rest rooms.
A long narrow passage lit with blinking fluorescence
Meanders into the Besser-brick entrails of the building.
Framed posters of consumerist decadence on peeling paint.
'Ah, a bookstore.'
Perhaps it has the new book
I heard about on the radio
In my 'next bookstore four hundred kilometres' rural home.
But no,
False pretences,
Book clearance centre in guise of 'nice rustic book emporium'.
Chainstores and bargain, clearance, retail outlets.
And walking like zombies,
Overloaded with Christmas shopping,
Those for whom this retail experience is normal.
Humanity on parade.
I make my escape,
With only a couple of completely superfluous purchases.
I feel almost dirty with the shame of it.
I am off to find a public park,
And a shady tree.

347: My Fergie

He's a classic,
Massey Ferguson 35X,
He is his original red,
But that doesn't make him racy.
He putts along at a walking pace,
As I slash the tussocks.
I am in low range,
Because the tussocks and cutty-grass are thick.
He can still give me a start when he picks up speed down hills
Or if one of his big wheels
Suddenly discovers a wombat hole.
Despite his loud hoarse monotone,
I find riding him,
In slowly diminishing circles,
Almost meditative.

Getting the PTO* into gear is a feat of agility.
I use the wrong foot to double clutch,
So the other is free
To whack the lever, grinding, into position.
With beings mechanically inanimate,
I have a precarious relationship,
Which means I am a poor driver.
I find the throttle, slasher raising, gear changing and braking
Sometimes beyond my motor planning.
But as I disengage the PTO,
Lower the slasher and pull on the brake,
I feel a real sense of achievement
That we have survived another excursion together.

* PTO: power take-off

349: Christmas Beetles

'Is that one, Mummy?'
'No, darling, that's just an ordinary little beetle.'
'But what do they look like?'
As I sit writing this prose, I spy
On the curtain
Its sharp little legs caught in circa 1950s
Lace curtain,
My fourth Christmas beetle of the year.
Three others were spotted encased in white silk
On the weather side of the kitchen window.
I noticed them in their haute couture shrouds
As I did the dishes.
Christmas beetles are a pleasant reminder
Of ghosts of Christmas past
When they cracked 'neath your thongs
As you ventured out across the veranda
For a nocturnal excursion to the outhouse.
Their whirring flutter past your face
As they headed for the porch light
Could be equally unnerving.
As children we'd befriend Christmas beetles,
And keep them in a matchbox.
We never really knew what to feed them,
So always shoved in some kikuyu.
Christmas beetles are large and scratchy.
You can hear them scrabble about on the timber floor.
They feel very tickly in your hand
If they are moving about.
I have found this sensation so uncomfortable
That I have dropped my little beetle onto the floor.

They are not brown, but they are.
They are not wholly green, but they are, in part.
Also blue and even a little reddish.
They are a browny, greeny, slightly bluey with a tinge of red
Shining opal colour.
Like an abalone shell.
Their presence is more Christmas to me
Than any California pine stuffed unceremonially
Into a sand-filled bucket.
And they're prettier too.

351: Procrastination or Disorganisation?

I just can't get my shit together.
It is taking an inordinate amount of time to organise
My bedroom, my house,
And my life in general.
I can see in my mind's eye how to do it.
But the details,
It is always the details,
Oh and the interruptions.
And then there are the wasted journeys
When you find yourself somewhere
And you can't remember why you were.
And the whole process is just so fatiguing
That you lie on the bedroom floor
And feel panicked at how much time has elapsed,
And how little you have achieved.
Being organised is my preferred state,
But getting organised is always a challenge.
I work very very hard at it.
I do not suffer from procrastination,
Just disorganisation.

353: Packing

Strewn,
Articles of clothing,
Packages which once contained
Toothpaste, insect repellent, socks.
Amidst this,
The detritus of everyday,
The clothes of yesterday,
Maintaining some of my body's shapes
Shedded vertically.
A cold cup of tea,
The cream a stagnant scum.
Bed unmade,
And around the room,
Piles,
In their multitudes.
Piles that make sense,
Like with like.
Piles that are a cacophony of clutter.
And beneath one of these,
My bags half packed.

356: Heat

In days pre-air-conditioning,
The populous,
Those wealthy enough,
Would escape to the cool climes of their mountain retreats.
But today,
It is hot even in the mountains,
Where we presently swelter.

We are of the less modern ilk,
And scorn such extravagances as reverse-cycle
Air conditioning.
We live off-grid.
So it is just hot.

No balmy sea breeze takes the edge off.
The water-tank-filled swimming pool
Is not even wading deep.
And the stagnant air is warm,
Beneath shady trees.

It is on these rare days,
Where lethargy and fractiousness reign,
And no productivity is possible,
That indolence and idleness should be embraced.

357: The Art of Delayed Gratification

According to the great sage of the twentieth century,
Edward P. Bear,
It is not in the actual eating of the honey
That the true pleasure is found.
It is in the anticipation of eating the honey.
Those moments before,
Where thoughts stray to
What eating honey shall be like.
Thoughts that are the culmination of
All prior pleasant experiences of eating honey,
With the heightened expectations
Of what this latest honey experience
May be like.

This is why, when expectations are not met,
For example if the honey jar is empty,
It can be so disappointing.
We cease to feel the pleasant feelings of anticipation.
Likewise;
If we have too much choice,
We also miss out on this wonderful feeling.
Where honey is on tap, for example,
There is no joy in anticipating eating honey.

Live in the moment and find joy?
Nup!
Discover the divine practice,
Of the Art of Delayed Gratification.
Practise temperance,
Be grateful,
And find healthy experiences to look forward to.

Honey in moderation.

358: My Cup Runneth Over

Today I am being gentle with myself.
My cup runneth over
With the fears and doubts,
The anxiety and regrets,
The slights and misunderstandings
Of all those I have been around.
I am a giant sponge
Who has absorbed their energy.
Now I am alone,
In quiet space,
To let it all out.
So perhaps then
I can be refilled
By being with those
Who have the vitality for living.

363: Something Missing

Some people have something missing.
It's a little gap,
In themselves.
Perhaps it is self-doubt.
Are they of value?
Are they here for a reason?

And this doubt
Creates a terrible gnawing inside
That drives them to despair
Or other desperate measures.
They cling to the edge of life,
With their knuckles whitening.

Mostly people fill this gap
With purpose.
A life of industry and usefulness.
Some fill it with acts of kindness.
Others with the care of partners and children.
They all see themselves reflected in their deeds,
And find their worth.

She trawls the internet looking for love
And pours out her sadness to strangers,
Hoping to find acceptance and approval.
I look on hopelessly.
She isn't courageous enough
To see the pattern of her folly.
And with each rejection,
Her gap increases.

www.ingramcontent.com/pod-product-compliance
Lightning Source LLC
Chambersburg PA
CBHW070900080526
44589CB00013B/1143